ZELDA'S
Survival Guide

Other Books by Carol Gardner and Shane Young

Zelda Wisdom
The Zen of Zelda
Zelda Rules on Love

Also by Carol Gardner

Bumper Sticker Wisdom

ZELDA'S
Survival Guide

Carol Gardner

Photographs by Shane Young

A Zelda Wisdom™ book

**Andrews McMeel
Publishing**

Kansas City

Zelda's Survival Guide

05 06 07 TWP 10 9 8 7 6 5 4 3

ISBN-13: 978-0-7407-3901-9
ISBN-10: 0-7407-3901-8

Library of Congress Control Number: 2003101083

ATTENTION: SCHOOLS AND BUSINESSES
Andrews McMeel books are available at quantity discounts with bulk
purchase for educational, business, or sales promotional use. For information,
please write to: Special Sales Department, Andrews McMeel Publishing,
4520 Main Street, Kansas City, Missouri 64111.

It is the loose ends
with which men hang themselves.

—Zelda Fitzgerald

The Key to survival is dogged determination.

Life is tough, but when it comes to survival what you need most is dogged determination and nobody knows more about dogged determination than a bulldog. Bulldogs are born with a nose that is slanted backward so they can breathe without letting go. Just try to take a bone away from me and you will discover how strong and stubborn I can be.

In putting Zelda's Survival Guide together, we started with a chapter on surviving childhood and parenting. Survival begins with birth, and babies seem to instinctively know how tough life is going to be. (Witness the fact that the first thing they do is cry!) In this chapter I teamed up with my puppy pal Angus to give you some tips on how to make it through those early years. Angus, as a ten-week-old puppy, was quite a sport, especially when it came to climbing all over me. For a little dog, Angus had big-dog attitude and it worked. When he wanted a toy, he held on to it, and in most cases, got and kept it. Sometimes it was touch and go: Angus would touch and I would go. With childhood and parenting it is often a toss-up as to who will survive, the child or the parent.

Surviving is a life-long process. People move from being dependent to being dependable. When they go to work the problems multiply. How do you survive in the work-a-day world? Again, the answer is dogged determination. You have to take risks, find your passion, work like a dog, watch your back, and yet still know how to work as a team player. One person is not a team.

The most difficult survival skills are needed when the hormones kick in. Love loss hurts and sometimes only humor, time, and, best of all, another love can heal a broken heart. In the chapter about surviving love loss my best friend, Baby, and I attempt to make you smile by showing you how to laugh at yourself and your situation. It isn't easy, but surviving a love loss is do-a-bull.

Just when you think you've survived childhood, parent-ing, the work-a-day world, and love loss, another tough phase shows up: midlife crisis, complete with wrinkles, weight gain, and gray hairs. Everything seems to be falling, including your spirits. The truth in the mirror and the reality that the past is gone and the future is uncertain gives us pause. The only thing to do is look life in the face and say, "I can win with a double chin." After all, growing old is the only way to live a long life.

Finally, I hope that in reading Zelda's Survival Guide you will let me be your guide dog. Survival is a skill we learn as we go, and how we go is what matters. If we can learn to laugh at ourselves, to be tough when necessary and ten-der when needed, and most of all to hang on after others let go . . . we will survive.

Some survive because they are destined to, but most survive because they are determined to.

—Zelda

Surviving

childhood and Parenting

Being a parent can be heavy. . .
very heavy.

Avoid the stumbling blocks
and the roadblocks.

Go for the building blocks.

Don't drink the bathwater.

Keeping it simple can be a lifesaver.

Learning how to lose is half the game.

To survive . . . it helps to be cute.

If you can't lick it . . . post it.

Learn all the rules . . . then break some.

A parent's best survival line:
"Because I said so!"

Surviving

the Work-a-Day World

It's not how hard you work . . .
it's how much work you get done.

The turtle only makes progress

when it sticks its neck out.

Failure to hit the bull's-eye
is not the fault of the target.

Survival is not about being brave
but about being chief.

Get all your ducks in a row.

Reality: Seeing your boss make a mistake.
Survival: Not mentioning it.

Snowflakes are fragile . . . but look what they can do when they stick together.

Believe in magic. Sometimes
you need to pull a rabbit out of a hat.

The worst day of fishing
beats the best day at work.

Housework won't kill you ...
but why risk it?

If all else fails . . . blame your computer.

Surviving

Love Loss

Love should be a snuggle . . .

not a struggle.

Love many, watch your back . . .
always paddle your own kayak.

#9730093

It is far better to have loved and lost ...

#9730633

than to have spent your whole life together.

Friends are life preservers.

Divorce: One usually gets the gold mine while the other gets the shaft.

Tears are a form of irrigation. Without tears we cannot grow.

Lose some.

Win some.

Love, honor, and negotiate.

Surviving

a Midlife Crisis

Currently surfing through midlife crisis.

Survival of the fittest.

You're never too old

to be young.

Overweight, wrinkles, double chin, flat chest, jowls, bloodshot eyes . . . if things don't improve, how will I get a date this weekend?

You know it's midlife crisis
when your chest falls into your drawers.

Face-lift? . . .
Do you think anyone will notice?

Life is uncertain.
Remember to eat your birthday cake
before you blow out the candles.

Just Surviving

(What It Takes to Hang in There)

Savor the sunny side of life.

Never argue with a skunk.

Survival depends on how high you can bounce back after you've hit bottom.

If you can laugh at yourself,
there will always be laughter in your life.

To survive in the jungle . . .
you can never wear too much leopard.

Know your enemy.

Survive with PEACE.

The happy camper's survival tip:
S'more is better.

Survival is hanging on after others let go.

I WILL survive!

Final survival advice:
Never, never, never give up!